ABC
OF FEELINGS

Baba, thanks for the paintbrush.
Mama, thanks for not making me code. —B.L.

PHILOMEL BOOKS

An imprint of Penguin Random House LLC, New York

First published in the United States of America by Philomel,
an imprint of Penguin Random House LLC, 2021

First published in Great Britain by Upside Down Books in 2020

Visit us online at penguinrandomhouse.com.

Library of Congress Cataloging-in-Publication Data is available.

Manufactured in China.

ISBN 9780593205198

1 3 5 7 9 10 8 6 4 2

Edited by Liza Kaplan.
Design by Monique Sterling.
Text set in Sentinel.

ABC OF FEELINGS

BONNIE LUI

PHILOMEL BOOKS

A is for **Anxious.**

Anxious is feeling really worried about something.

B is for **Brave.**

Brave is being nervous
about something . . .

. . . and doing it anyway!

 **is for Curious.**

Curious is seeking answers
to all your questions.

D is for **Determined.**

Determined is when nothing can stop you.

is for **Embarrassed.**

Embarrassed is feeling worried and upset about something you don't want other people to notice.

is for **Foolish.**

Foolish is feeling absolutely, positively ridiculous.

G is for **Grateful.**

Grateful is feeling thankful for what you have.

H is for **Happy.**

Happy is when everything
feels wonderful!

I is for **Insecure.**

Insecure is feeling a bit
wobbly inside.

J is for **Jealous.**

Jealous is wanting what someone else has.

K is for **Kind.**

Kind is being good and thoughtful toward others.

is for **Lonely.**

Lonely is feeling sad about being alone.

M is for **Mad.**

Mad is feeling super-duper
MEGA angry!

N is for Needy.

Needy is wanting someone you love to pay attention to you.

O

is for **Overwhelmed.**

Overwhelmed is having too many
thoughts and feelings all at once.

P is for **Powerful.**

Powerful is feeling strong and able.

Q is for **Quiet.**

Quiet is being calm and peaceful.

R is for **Restless.**

Restless is feeling like you cannot relax.

CAMP

S is for **Scared.**

Scared is being very
afraid of something.

 is for **Trusting.**

Trusting is feeling safe with someone.

U is for **Unhappy.**

Unhappy is when you are very sad.

V is for **Vulnerable.**

Vulnerable is opening your heart
to show the world how you feel.

 **is for Wishful.**

Wishful is hoping something magical will happen!

X is for **Xenial.**

Xenial is being welcoming to strangers.

**Y** is for **Yearning.**

Yearning is really,

really,

really

wanting something.

Z is for **Zany.**

Zany is being funny, wacky . . .

and uniquely YOU!

A    B   C   D

Anxious   Brave   Curious   Determined

J   K   L   M

Jealous   Kind   Lonely   Mad

S   T   U   V

Scared   Trusting   Unhappy   Vulnerable

E
Embarrassed

F
Foolish

G
Grateful

H
Happy

I
Insecure

N
Needy

O
Overwhelmed

P
Powerful

Q
Quiet

R
Restless

W
Wishful

X
Xenial

Y
Yearning

Z
Zany

It is imperative to a child's well-being to teach them about all of the emotions, allow them to feel and express them, and give them the tools to manage these feelings. *ABC of Feelings* is a book that provides young readers with an important framework upon which to build a future of strong mental health. This book has been handpicked by our specialist team at Upside Down Books with the purpose of introducing children to a wide-ranging emotional vocabulary. I hope you enjoy *ABC of Feelings* as much as my family and I do.

Lauren Callaghan
Consultant Clinical Psychologist,
Cofounder and Clinical Director of Trigger Publishing